(un)Reasonable Trust

The Book of Habakkuk

Nate Holdridge

Paperback ISBN: 9798215164341

Ebook ISBN: 9798215315712

First paperback edition September 2022

Edited by Elsa Dooling and Anne Jensen

Cover Art by BK Designs (bklingenberg.com)

Audiobook Engineering by Daniel Reed

nateholdridge.com

Contents

To my firstborn daughter, Lauren. May God reveal himself to you as you sit on your watchtower.

1

Problem (Habakkuk 1)

The book *Dune* is set in the distant future. In one early scene, a young Paul Atreides is interrogated by a witch who represents a religious sect that helps rule the universe. She forces him to put his hand in a box that mysteriously produces terrible pain without damaging the flesh. She is testing him to see how he responds to suffering. At first, he winces and screams, but he holds his composure and determines not to withdraw his hand. He becomes resolved to endure pain.

At the end of the short book of Habakkuk, the prophet said that even if all the crops in Israel were to yield no produce and even if all the livestock in Israel died off, he would rejoice and take joy in God (Habakkuk 3:17-18). Even if the earth suffered chaos in apocalyptic proportions, Habakkuk would trust God. God had made him strong, so he would move forward, trusting God despite all he saw, despite the pain of his hand in the box (Habakkuk 3:19). At the end of the book, Habakkuk demonstrates remarkable trust in God.

That is how the book ends, not how it begins. At the start of his book, Habakkuk was reeling. He questioned God. He was upset at God. And he longed to know what God was doing because, from Habakkuk's perspective, God was not doing anything.

So what happened that took this man from despair to trust? A conversation with God—a conversation recorded in these three brief chapters. In their dialogue together, Habakkuk fixates on a problem as he saw it, God gives a promise to Habakkuk and the world, and Habakkuk then praises God for what he heard—concluding with a strong song of faith. The conversation changes Habakkuk. He progressed from worry to worship and from fear to faith.

Because of this progression, I have given this book on Habakkuk the title *Unreasonable/Reasonable Trust*. I pray it helps us develop a trust in God that is not based on reasons we can see with our own eyes or logic (unreasonable, or without reasons), but a trust that is based on his nature (reasonable, or with reasons).

A Song of Discouragement (1:1-4)

"The oracle that Habakkuk the prophet saw. O LORD, how long shall I cry for help, and you will not hear? Or cry to you 'Violence!' and you will not save? Why do you make me see iniquity, and why do you idly look at wrong? Destruction and violence are before me; strife and contention arise. So the law is paralyzed,

and justice never goes forth. For the wicked surround the righteous; so justice goes forth perverted." (Habakkuk 1:1–4)

A Burdened Prophet

We might not know Habakkuk's backstory, but this quick introduction tells us a lot about him. First, we suspect he was a poetic man because this beginning statement is written in song form. And our suspicions will be confirmed in the final chapter of his book—there, he wrote a prayer to a song style called a Shigionoth and gave instructions to the choirmaster to play it on stringed instruments (Habakkuk 3:1, 19).

Second, we learn he was a burdened man. He'd seen an **oracle**, a word meaning "what is lifted up" and that some translate as "burden." Receiving an oracle meant Habakkuk had received a prophetic vision from God, and that vision burdened his heart. Like a soldier with an eighty-pound pack on his back, Habakkuk's every movement was slowed by the presence of his burden.

Third, right away, we must note that he felt free to be brutally honest with God. He wonders aloud how long he's going to have to pray. He wonders if God hears him. He is tired of alerting God to the violence all around him without any response. He challenges God's wisdom, asking him why he has to see so much sin. He is frustrated by all the destruction, violence, strife, and contention all around him. He even tells God that the Bible is ineffective—justice never happens, and the wicked keep multiplying! And when justice is administered, it's clumsy, and a cheap imitation of true justice.

But this last note about the prophet helps us learn something about God. Habakkuk's prayer made it into the Bible. God did not order a ban on Habakkuk's questions. He welcomed them and—as we will learn in a moment—gave a shocking response to them.

Hints at the Setting

Just as we can learn a bit about Habakkuk and his God from this opening salvo, we can also glean a little about the situation that made Habakkuk write this song in the first place. The key is found in his conclusion that **the law is paralyzed**.

What this helps us understand is the location of all the despairing things Habakkuk saw. As a prophet who was concerned with God's people—the church of that era—Habakkuk desperately wanted God's word to regulate the lives of God's people. He taught and prophesied and sang with the hopes that God's congregation would submit to God's law.

But the law was paralyzed—among God's children. The odds are strong that all this happened after the reign of King Josiah. Josiah had been a good king who led a revival of the worship of God in Israel. But the reform must have been only a top-down, outward, legislated one rather than a bottom-up, heartfelt, personal one because the second Josiah died, the people drifted back into disobedience. For a hot minute, the king compelled them to worship God, but once the king was dead, their true hearts were revealed.

Habakkuk didn't start his book bemoaning the sin outside Israel, but the sin inside Israel. Perhaps you can relate. There are many elements of today's society that discourage believers. *But a mature believer is more disturbed by sin inside the church than outside it.*

Who was Habakkuk saddened and frustrated by? Not the world. But God's church. This is one of the most important interpretive questions to get right with this book. It is tempting to use the book of Habakkuk as a soapbox against society's ills—and many have done so—but Habakkuk was initially discouraged by the ills of God's people. To use Habakkuk to rail against sin in the world is like being in the emergency room with a gunshot wound to the stomach, getting out of your bed, going across the hall, reading your neighbor's chart, and becoming upset about their sprained ankle. Read your own charts! There is plenty to be sad about right there. Habakkuk had, and all he saw broke his heart.

The law was simply paralyzed. What a picture! A dead body part is lifeless, but a paralyzed body part has life, but not ability. The designed function of a paralyzed hand is clear, but the paralysis keeps it from doing what it was designed to do. And, as Habakkuk looked out at Israel, he felt the law was not able to do what it was designed to do. Something in God's people paralyzed the living Word of God!

In our age of church scandals, the prevalence of strange doctrines, and a general acknowledgment that many Christians do not look any different from the world they are living in, can we not relate? It can feel like the word is paralyzed to work among God's people—all the pornography, all the consumerism, all the self-expression, and all the hyper-independence seem to keep the positive effects of the Bible from breaking into many lives. Habakkuk saw it and asked *how long?* Perhaps we ask the same.

It is important to acknowledge, however, that Jesus saw and did more than Habakkuk (or we) ever could. Jesus saw the depths of our sin and depravity, the total enslavement of our souls to unrighteousness. And he was able to do more than merely bemoan what he saw—he acted. What he saw, though repulsive, made him run to us, not away from us. Because of what Jesus saw, he offered more than a complaint. He offered a solution. He came with his cross to save us.

The book does not end with Habakkuk's initial flurry of emotion. The song continues. The direction of the language changes here—this next section is penned by God.

––––––––––

A Surprising Discipline (1:5-11)

"Look among the nations, and see; wonder and be astounded. For I am doing a work in your days that you would not believe if told. For behold, I am raising up the Chaldeans, that bitter and hasty nation, who march through the breadth of the earth, to seize dwellings not their own. They are dreaded and fearsome; their justice and dignity go forth from themselves. Their horses are swifter than leopards, more fierce than the evening wolves; their horsemen press proudly on. Their horsemen come from afar; they fly like an eagle swift to devour. They all come for violence, all their faces forward. They gather captives like sand. At kings they scoff, and at rulers they laugh. They laugh at every fortress, for they pile up earth and take it. Then they sweep by like the wind and go on, guilty men, whose own might is their god!"
(Habakkuk 1:5–11)

The Chaldeans

That God answered Habakkuk might have startled the prophet—many Jewish songs of mourning never got a response. But God was already working on something before Habakkuk uttered his lyrics, so now God is ready to sing about all he is doing. But what did God's song say?

It said God was about to do an astounding work Habakkuk would have trouble believing. It predicted that in Habakkuk's lifetime, God would raise up the wicked and violent Chaldean armies to invade Israel. It acknowledged that these Chaldeans answered to no man and were a law unto themselves. It spoke of their speed, ferocity, and pride by comparing them to leopards, wolves, and horsemen. It compared the number of their captives to innumerable sands. And it detailed their response to kings and fortresses that tried to obstruct them—all they did was laugh before mowing them down! Finally, God sang that they swept through like a hurricane and worshipped their own military might and power.

If Habakkuk's song was like a moody and despairing Nirvana track, God's song was like a jarring and confrontational Rage Against the Machine one. Habakkuk might have mourned the sin of God's people, but God was tired of mourning for so many years. He had already sent prophet after prophet to his people, calling them to turn and repent. Now—after half a millennium of patience—it was time for action.

He would send the Chaldeans to wake up his slumbering people. You might know the Chaldeans as what they eventually developed into—the Babylonians. When King Nebuchadnezzar and his Babylonian forces did finally invade Judah, they were merciless—just as God had said to Habakkuk. Their brutality can be illustrated by what they did to the last king of Judah. After a long siege against Jerusalem, the Babylonians took King Zedekiah, slaughtered his prince-sons, and gouged out his eyes before delivering him to a Babylonian prison (1 Kings 25:1-7).

And—do not miss this—God's lyrics are abundantly poetic in nature. It is like God in heaven sat down at his desk with pen in hand to write down his deliberate poem of discipline. Why is this important? Because it tells us God was not writing in cold prose about the hard facts of his judgment. He used the art and romance of poetry to express his heart. It was planned and calculated but also sad and heartfelt. He is not a prosecuting lawyer building a case but a jilted lover who cannot believe it has come to this.

And this poem-song is a shock! God would cure his people's disobedience by sending seemingly worse people to chasten them. The Chaldeans would be God's scalpel to help him access the cancer deep within Israel. Like a jilted lover, it is as if God will do anything—even the most extreme things—to rescue his people. Like the hero in every modern Liam Neeson movie, God will take any measure necessary to win us back to himself.

God's Unbelievable Work

God's ways are not our ways. Here, we see this truth as Habakkuk and God's perspectives are placed in stark contrast. God's way of sending the Chaldeans was high above Habakkuk's desire for another reform or revival. And when God tells Habakkuk what he is going to do, it is like a mathematical genius trying to explain calculus to a little child who has only learned simple addition. This is why God said Habakkuk would not believe it. He could not. To him, it did not add up.

We are often this way. We have our simple equations for things like the presence of evil or human suffering. We have questions about why evil flourishes. But we often approach these questions with a simple addition of what *we* think is good or what *we* think is bad. God, however, approaches these problems with the calculus of the gospel, consuming the worst of evils on the cross so that all who believe in Jesus can escape all pain forever. But it is often hard for us to process because we are like children in comparison to the wisdom of God.

And though this work was hard for Habakkuk to believe, we should believe it. Christians, of all people, understand that death precedes resurrection. And God's people needed some resurrecting in Habakkuk's day, so God was going to allow some death. As Jesus said:

> *"Every branch in me that does not bear fruit he takes away, and every branch that does bear fruit he prunes, that it may bear more fruit."*
> (John 15:2)

Israel needed a bit of pruning before better fruit could come. When Peter wrote to a church that was suffering because they were being marginalized, he said God was using it to sharpen his people:

> *"For it is time for judgment to begin at the household of God..."* (1 Peter 4:17)

Perhaps we are also shocked today that God would choose to work in this way. Perhaps we cannot imagine God using wicked schemes, worldviews, or movements to discipline his people. But why not? Why can God not shape us in that way?

Well, Habakkuk might have been shocked by God's response-song, but that did not mean he would be silent. He had something to say about it.

A Statement of Disillusionment (1:12-17)

"Are you not from everlasting, O LORD my God, my Holy One? We shall not die. O LORD, you have ordained them as a judgment, and you, O Rock, have established them for reproof. You who are of purer eyes than to see evil and cannot look at wrong, why do you idly look at traitors and remain silent when the wicked swallows up the man more righteous than he? You make mankind like the fish of the sea, like crawling things that have no ruler. He brings all of them up with a hook; he drags them out with his net; he gathers them in his dragnet; so he rejoices and is glad. Therefore he sacrifices to his net and makes offerings to his dragnet; for by them he lives in luxury, and his food is rich. Is he then to keep on emptying his net and mercilessly killing nations forever?" (Habakkuk 1:12–17)

I Thought

Habakkuk's rebuttal was a statement of disillusionment. He had three beliefs that made him confused by God's promise of discipline at the hands of the Chaldeans.

First, he had always thought of the Chaldeans as evil people who were ordained for judgment and correction. If anyone needed discipline, Habakkuk thought, it was them! They were brutal, treating the nations like fishermen treat fish, catching them in their net before feasting on their lives.

Second, he had thought Israel was special. He said to God, "We shall not die. We are more righteous than them." He did not understand that, as God's people, God's expectation of them was higher than it was for nonbelievers.

Third, he thought God was a good God. God was from another perfect and holy dimension. He thought God could not even look at evil—and certainly, the Chaldeans were evil.

Perhaps you have been where Habakkuk was—trying to reconcile different concepts you thought you knew about God. Maybe you have even done what Habakkuk did and tried to argue with God by appealing to a facet of God's character—*God, you are love, so you should do this! God, you are holy, so you should do this!*

It all seemed so strange (and maybe excessive) to Habakkuk, and he had theological arguments ready to go. He shot back at God, reminding God that he is holy, just, and good—how could he allow the sin of the Chaldeans to go unchecked? No longer was Habakkuk concerned about sin within the camp but outside it. Surely these wicked murderers deserved more of God's judgment than Habakkuk's people did!

Habakkuk felt God's medicine was worse than the disease. The prophet would have preferred another reform or revival in the land—he had experienced one a few years earlier. *If only we could go through another revival,* Habakkuk thought, *it would stick this time!*

Habakkuk felt like many of us do—that evil is pointless. God had a specific plan for using the wicked Chaldeans in the life of his people—and that plan is difficult for us to imagine. But just because we cannot imagine a good reason why God might allow something to happen does not mean there cannot be one. We are doing basic addition, but God is busy doing advanced calculus. As Tim Keller wrote in his seminal book, The Reason For God:

> *"If you have a God great and transcendent enough to be mad at because he hasn't stopped evil and suffering in the world, then you have (at the same moment) a God great and transcendent enough to have good reasons for allowing it to continue that you can't know. Indeed, you can't have it both ways."*[1]

The Cross

The cross of Christ shows us that God is love and holy, just and merciful. It also shows us that—in God's estimation—the only true way to eradicate evil is not by putting the world on autopilot so he can do whatever he wants at a given moment but by going himself to suffer, die, and rise from the dead.

We must remember this about God. Habakkuk was stressed out because the Chaldeans were treating the nations like fishermen treat fish. But we must remember that God went fishing too. He sent his Son so that all who would believe in him would no longer perish but enter into abundant life (John 3:16).

When children play tag, they often have a home base. It is a place of safety. For believers, going back to the cross of Christ is our place of safety, especially when life is confusing.

Habakkuk will not remain in his state of confusion forever. After completing this first step of presenting the problem (as he saw it) to God, Habakkuk would go on to listen to what God had to say. God will promise judgment on all unrighteousness and evil one day. And, in response to God's promise, Habakkuk will praise God for his faithfulness. After praise, Habakkuk will arrive at a position of deep trust in God. For Habakkuk—and many believers over the centuries—the equation is simple: The Problem + God's Promises ⼀ Our Praise = Trust.

This trust is the goal, but often we get stuck on the problem. Why is there evil in the world or, more egregiously, in the church? Why do people who claim to love God sometimes behave the way they do? Why is there not more love and devotion to God and his word? Why do insidious ideologies and movements gain traction in our modern times? Why do people get sick without cause? Why can we not shake ourselves from war and famine and disease? Why do innocent children suffer and die? Why? Why? Why? With all these questions, we can quickly get stuck on the problem. Soon, we become unable to move forward into the kind of trust that can get us through life and into a kingdom without problems of any kind.

It was hard for Habakkuk to believe that God would win over his people through their defeat at the hands of the Chaldeans. When these Chaldeans invaded Israel, it looked like Israel lost, when actually, it was a great triumph and an important step for God's people.

Similarly, when we look back on Jesus' life, we know that God won the victory over sin by being crushed in death on the cross. We know that at the moment it appeared that God lost the battle, he was winning it. We know that the Son consumed wrath far worse than the Chaldeans could bring. Yet his death is what brought us life.

No, we should not be surprised at all that God might work in this way. To Habakkuk, God said, "I am doing a work in your days that you would not believe if told" (Habakkuk 1:5). Paul even applied this quote to the gospel—what God did on the cross is unimaginably good and hard to believe when you hear it! (see Acts 13:37-41). But we have been told of God's marvelous work in our days—and praise God, many of us have believed!

---

1. Keller, Timothy. 2008. The Reason for God. Dutton Books.

2

Promise (Habakkuk 2)

"I will take my stand at my watchpost and station myself on the tower, and look out to see what he will say to me, and what I will answer concerning my complaint. And the Lord answered me: 'Write the vision; make it plain on tablets, so he may run who reads it. For still the vision awaits its appointed time; it hastens to the end—it will not lie. If it seems slow, wait for it; it will surely come; it will not delay. Behold, his soul is puffed up; it is not upright within him, but the righteous shall live by his faith. Moreover, wine is a traitor, an arrogant man who is never at rest. His greed is as wide as Sheol; like death he has never enough. He gathers for himself all nations and collects as his own all peoples.'" (Habakkuk 2:1–5).

The Righteous Will Live by His Faith

Many of us love the idea of the courtroom. We love our courtroom dramas and movies, along with real, live courtroom TV. We love watching the accused squirm in their seat. We love the tension of the moment.

At this point in Habakkuk, God has been called to Habakkuk's courtroom. The prophet has questioned God's goodness, wisdom, and holiness. He wonders why God is going to send the Babylonian armies to invade Israel and how that could be a just decision. Everyone knows the Babylonians are ruthless and evil. How could God allow them to run rampant over the nations?

The main idea of this passage is that God makes a promise to Habakkuk—and the world—that Babylon and all who imitate her will one day answer to God for the evil they have committed. God responds here to Habakkuk's accusations by assuring him that Babylon's crimes will not go unpunished.

Through five woes of judgment, God detailed the evil of Babylon better than Habakkuk did. But before those woes, God summarized Babylon: **his soul is puffed up, it is not upright within him** (4). Like a bloated toad, Babylon was filled with self-assurance and pride. They thought no one could overcome them and that they could have their way with the societies of the earth. But God saw their hubris and pledged to execute justice on them.

If that is the future of the wicked, what about the righteous? God also had a summary for them: **the righteous will live by his faith** (4). Many of you know this is a significant statement in Christianity. The New Testament writers quoted it often as a way to explain that we can only become righteous in God's sight through belief in the gospel and that after saving faith should want to live in continual trust in God (Galatians 3:11,

Romans 1:17, Hebrews 10:38). And in the sixteenth century, this verse aided Martin Luther in his departure from Roman Catholicism. One day, as a pilgrim in Rome, Luther visited a staircase the church said was miraculously transported from Pontius Pilate's judgment hall in Jerusalem. The custom for pilgrims was to get on their knees and crawl up the harsh stone steps, kissing stains the church claimed were left by Christ's blood. As Luther was crawling, this statement that the righteous will live by their faith popped into his mind. He realized he was trying to work his way to God when no work would do. He realized salvation and life before God comes by faith. He got up, left for his home in Germany, and became a major contributor to the reformation. He was free!

For the original readers, the faith God described meant trusting God's plan to judge Israel with the Babylonian armies and believing what God said about Babylon's ultimate destiny. Even when they were in exile 600 miles from Jerusalem, they needed to be confident that God was not done with his people. Though it looked like the world and its powers were winning while God and his people were losing, the righteous live by faith that the opposite is true. The world and its powers would—and will—face an ultimate day of reckoning.

This brand of faith produces a solid steadfastness in you. It is a faith that leads to faithfulness—a strong conviction that God is worth following no matter what unfolds around you. It generates an assurance and confidence about God's unseen promises (Hebrews 11:1). It generates an Abel-like thankfulness to God (Hebrews 11:4). It generates an Enoch-like walk with God (Hebrews 11:5-6). It generates a Noah-like obedience to God (Hebrews 11:7). It generates an Abraham-like endurance that waits for God (Hebrews 11:8-12) It generates a Sarah-like patience that submits to God (Hebrews 11:11). It generates an Isaac-like submission to God (Hebrews 11:20). It generates a Jacob-like desire for the blessing of God (Hebrews 11:21). It generates a Joseph-like anticipation of the permanent future city of God (Hebrews 11:22). This type of faith produces a beautiful brand of life in us. So how can we develop this level of trust? This chapter shows us three ways.

Patiently Wait (2:1-5)

Watchtower

First, the passage shows us we must patiently wait for God. Habakkuk began realizing this right after his diatribe against God in the first chapter. He said, **"I will take my stand at my watchpost and station myself on the tower, and look out to see what he will say to me, and what I will answer concerning my complaint"** (Habakkuk 2:1). The prophet had a sense that he needed to wait for God's corrective word—his divine perspective—so he went to his proverbial watchtower and waited for God to speak.

The concept of a prophet in a watchtower is a biblical one (Isaiah 21:6-12, Ezekiel 23:17-21, Hosea 9:8). But Habakkuk's first step is one we can also take. When our reasoning with God or arguments against God take us as far as they can, when we become stuck on the problem as we see it, we need to patiently wait for instruction. We must go to our watchtower and wait for God.

A watchtower is elevated above the place it protects, and we need places that detach us from the regular flow of life so we can get perspective and help. We need our Bibles, our churches, and our prayer closets to provide watchtower moments. Like a student stuck on a problem, hand raised, waiting for the help of a tutor or teacher, we must raise our hand and begin looking for God's perspective.

Tablets

As Habakkuk waited, God began to answer. Before giving his full perspective, God said, **"Write the vision; make it plain on tablets, so he may run who reads it"** (Habakkuk 2:2). Habakkuk would have understood that God wanted him to write down everything he said so that prophetic runners could take the message of God to God's people. God wanted everyone in Israel to know that though the Chaldean-Babylonian army was coming to discipline Israel, he would one day execute judgment on them. Then, as God's people heard God's word, they were to run in the truth God declared.

Daniel is a good example of an Israelite who ran with the vision God spoke to Habakkuk. During long years in Babylon, Daniel trusted that God's story was not finished and that one day his kingdom would come. He ran in the understanding that, as powerful as Nebuchadnezzar and all the kings after him were, their power would not last forever. One day, God would establish his forever kingdom and reign without end.

This is another fine way to patiently wait for God—get into his word. Get further clarity on his truth and promises. Cling to them so that you can run through life with the correct mentality.

Trail race organizers understand the importance of learning what is coming in advance. Race websites will post the route, along with all the elevation shifts the runner should expect. This way, the informed runner knows when the big hills are coming and can prepare accordingly. And as we sit with God's word, we learn what the course is like. We find out what is coming, where this is all going, and how we should respond.

Slow-Moving Justice

Another way we should patiently wait is with...patience. God told Israel what would happen to Babylon, and it seems this is what is going to happen to the world system as well. In Revelation 17-18, we learn that another Babylon will be destroyed right before Christ returns. I think it is imagery that describes the destruction of the world system that is in dominance today. But it is taking a long time to get there, just as it took a while for the original Babylon to face its judgment. Some have called this God's slow-moving justice, and this justice requires patience.

But we do not like to wait. There is an example of this impatience in the book of Jeremiah. He had said things similar to Habakkuk but in greater detail and with a more prophetic flourish. One day, with a farming yoke made for oxen on his neck, Jeremiah announced that the Babylonians would yoke the people into slavery for seventy years. But a false prophet named Hananiah was there, and he took the yoke off Jeremiah's neck, broke it, and told everyone that God would break Babylon in the space of two years. When confronted with decades of captivity or two years of difficulty, the people believed Hananiah. They did not want to imagine a long process of waiting for God to rescue them (Jeremiah 28). But we must not be like them. Instead, we should trust in God's slow-moving justice.

In 1967, singer-songwriter Bob Dylan recorded and released his song, *All Along The Watchtower* (a song Jimi Hendrix covered the next year). The song is a conversation between two horse riders—a joker and a thief. The joker complains that businessmen were thieving from him without consequence. Many have thought the concept for the song was lifted from Isaiah 21, a passage that likely inspired Habakkuk. In it, God tells Isaiah to get on the watchtower to witness the future fall of Babylon. The idea is simple: though we see and experience injustice and evil, one day, God will settle all accounts. But we must climb the watchtower, find God's promises of judgment in his word, and patiently wait for that day to come.

———

Sing the Woes (2:6-20)

The Woes

Another way the passage shows us to live by faith is to sing the five woes God pronounced over evil Babylon. Before thinking about each woe, I want you to notice something important—God is not the singer, but those waiting for justice are. God said, **"Shall not these take up their taunt against (Babylon), with scoffing and riddles for him?"** (Habakkuk 2:6). What this means is that the Israelites and other nations that Babylon had destroyed were meant to sing this battle rap of woe with the confidence that God would defend them. And just as they sang it over historical Babylon, the child of God can sing this song over the spiritual system of Babylon today. We can rejoice that one day all oppression and violence and greed and sensuality and idolatry will be destroyed.

But what did they sing?

"Shall not all these take up their taunt against him, with scoffing and riddles for him, and say, 'Woe to him who heaps up what is not his own—for how long?—and loads himself with pledges!' Will not your debtors suddenly arise, and those awake who will make you tremble? Then you will be spoil for them. Because you have plundered many nations, all the remnant of the peoples shall plunder you, for the blood of man and violence to the earth, to cities and all who dwell in them." (Habakkuk 2:6–8)

In this first woe, they sang that the plunderer would be plundered. Babylon had taken nations—their wealth, land, and peoples—that did not belong to them. They had plundered, but one day they would be plundered. The Babylonians had thought they were robbing the bank over and over, but God said they were actually taking out loans over and over. One day, they would pay.

"Woe to him who gets evil gain for his house, to set his nest on high, to be safe from the reach of harm! You have devised shame for your house by cutting off many peoples; you have forfeited your life. For the stone will cry out from the wall, and the beam from the woodwork respond." (Habakkuk 2:9–11)

This second woe of the song says that the one harming will eventually suffer harm. God depicted them as birds trying to set their nest on high so they could be out of harm's reach. Everyone is entitled to build and save and prosper, but these

Babylonians created their secure position by destabilizing other peoples and nations. God said even the **stones** and **beams** they stole from other lands would testify against them.

> *"Woe to him who builds a town with blood and founds a city on iniquity! Behold, is it not from the LORD of hosts that peoples labor merely for fire, and nations weary themselves for nothing? For the earth will be filled with the knowledge of the glory of the LORD as the waters cover the sea."* (Habakkuk 2:12–14)

This third woe of the song says that the oppressor would end up with nothing. They had **built their towns** and **founded their cities** with the blood of laborers and slaves who were given no choice in the matter (12). God said building a society that way was like building a bonfire—it feels like you are getting somewhere, but it will soon be burned to ash (12). All their efforts would be lost. Their future was nothingness.

> *"Woe to him who makes his neighbors drink— you pour out your wrath and make them drunk, in order to gaze at their nakedness! You will have your fill of shame instead of glory. Drink, yourself, and show your uncircumcision! The cup in the LORD's right hand will come around to you, and utter shame will come upon your glory! The violence done to Lebanon will over- whelm you, as will the destruction of the beasts that terrified them, for the blood of man and violence to the earth, to cities and all who dwell in them."* (Habakkuk 2:15–17)

This fourth woe of the song says that those who promote rampant sensuality would be exposed. God said they used alcohol to get their neighbors **drunk**, all with the goal of increasing nakedness (15). This was God's way of saying that this Babylonian society and system promotes sensuality and sexual expression that defies God, using alcohol and substances to get there. But God saw all their violence—including the violence they did to the forests and animal species of **Lebanon**—and would judge it (16-17).

> *"What profit is an idol when its maker has shaped it, a metal image, a teacher of lies? For its maker trusts in his own creation when he makes speechless idols! Woe to him who says to a wooden thing, Awake; to a silent stone, Arise! Can this teach? Behold, it is overlaid with gold and silver, and there is no breath at all in it. But the LORD is in his holy temple; let all the earth keep silence before him."* (Habakkuk 2:18–20)

This last woe of the song says that those who try to make their own gods will one day hear the voice of the true God. A major reason someone invents their own religion is so they can tell their "gods" what to say, but the true God will have the final word.

Each woe is worth our contemplation today. In each, the actions of Babylon should make us sorrowful, but to our sorrow, we can add the joy of knowing God will right every wrong.

The movies understand this song. When the villain or bully or unjust or cheater is revealed, the audience begins hoping for their demise. We want them to get what is coming to them. And, often, that is precisely the way the script plays out. In under three hours, justice is served. But this song helps us wait with patience for the justice God promises to deliver. It is coming.

In the classic book Anne of Green Gables, the main character, Anne, a feisty, red-headed orphan adopted by a hardened but loving woman named Marilla, asked Marilla if she had ever seen someone outgrow their red hair. When Marilla said no, Anne said, *"Well, that is another hope gone. 'My life is a perfect graveyard of buried hopes.'"*[1] This is true without the gospel. With the gospel, however, our lives can become fertile ground for hope to grow. The seeds of injustice, greed, violence, sensuality, and idolatry go in, but out comes the hope that God will deal with it all one day when Christ returns. Because of Jesus, despair is the fertile ground of hope.

Be Filled With Wonder (2:14, 20)

The Earth's Destiny

This fertile ground is all hinted at in the passage. God said, **"For the earth will be filled with the knowledge of the glory of the Lord as the waters cover the sea"** (Habakkuk 2:14). God said the same thing to Isaiah (Isaiah 11:9). And right here, smack in the middle of all five woes, God declares a day is coming when the whole world will know and love God. When Jesus came, he brought the beginnings of this kingdom. It is already here but not yet fully revealed.

For that full revelation, we wait. Confronted with a world and culture that is often hostile to Christianity, we have the strong confidence that a day is coming when God will be loved by everyone. But, like Abraham, we must faithfully wait for it, looking forward in awe-filled wonder. As Hebrews said:

> *"By faith he went to live in the land of promise, as in a foreign land, living in tents with Isaac and Jacob, heirs with him of the same promise. For he was looking forward to the city that has foundations, whose designer and builder is God."* (Hebrews 11:9–10)

Keep Silence

We are often like little children in the back of the SUV—*Dad, are we there yet? How long until we get there?* For this feeling, God gave Habakkuk (and us) a wise practice. In his last word in Habakkuk, God said, **"The Lord is in his holy temple; let all the earth keep silence before him"** (20).

This exhortation is in direct contrast with what came before it. God said the Babylonians made idols that could not speak. The Babylonians could say whatever they wanted to their gods without any hope of a response. But we must be silent because God speaks—he is alive, working, promising, and judging.

Like Habakkuk, we can replace our complaints and doubts with the firm expectation that God will come and establish his kingdom.

In a classic scene from C.S. Lewis' *The Lion, The Witch and the Wardrobe,* Mr. and Mrs. Beaver play emergency host to the

Pevensie children. Peter, Susan, Edmund, and Lucy had discovered the magical world of Narnia, and the talking beavers helped them acclimate. While they talked, the beavers let slip that their world was under a witch's curse and that she had the power to turn her enemies to stone, but that they were awaiting the return of Aslan, a fierce lion who would defeat her in battle. Edmund asked, *"Won't she turn him into stone too?"*

Mrs. Beaver replied, *"Turn him into stone!? If she can stand on her two feet and look him in the face, it'll be the most she can do and more than I expect of her. No, no. He'll put all to rights, as it says in an old rhyme in these parts:*

Wrong will be right, when Aslan comes in sight, At the sound of his roar, sorrows will be no more, When he bares his teeth, winter meets its death, And when he shakes his mane, we shall have spring again."[2]

A major facet of the Christian life is our questioning of evil and injustice in the world. What is God doing? When will he react?

Like Habakkuk, we must trust God's promise. Just as Mr. and Mrs. Beaver awaited Aslan, we must await God's wise, certain, and successful judgment of all evil. We must believe a day is coming when the knowledge of his glory will cover the earth as the waters cover the sea. His fame will run from pole to pole, and every nation, culture, and society will be allegiant to his name. And, in trusting silence, we must wait for that day when Christ comes to rule the nations with a rod of iron (Revelation 12:5, 19:15), when the lion will lie down with the lamb (Isaiah 11:6, 65:25), and when the whole world will flow to his house in adoration and worship (Micah 4:1).

---

1. Montgomery, L. M. 2017. Anne of Green Gables. London, England: Arcturus Publishing.

2. Lewis, C. S. 2009. The Lion, the Witch and the Wardrobe. London, England: HarperCollins.

3

Praise (Habakkuk 3:1-16)

"A prayer of Habakkuk the prophet, according to Shigionoth. 'O LORD, I have heard the report of you, and your work, O LORD, do I fear. In the midst of the years revive it; in the midst of the years make it known; in wrath remember mercy.'" (Habakkuk 3:1–2).

Songs impact us. Some music can aid concentration. Some music is great for relaxation. Some music is perfect for a road trip, while other music belongs in a gym. There's a reason we play Reggae at the beach and do not play Mozart during CrossFit. Songs impact us.

The prayer before us is a song about God. It includes three moments of musical pause and reflection called a **"Selah"** (Habakkuk 3, 9, 13). Habakkuk said it was meant to be played **according to Shigionoth**, which seems to relate to a word meaning "reel to and fro." The musical clues mean this song might have been played to a chaotic beat, perhaps to reflect the swirling impact of God's words on Habakkuk's mind.

But, as wild as this song might have sounded to the original hearers, it ends with calm hope and trust in God. Though Habakkuk did not understand everything, he hoped in God. How can this hope develop? How did Habakkuk go from a tumultuous song to a soothed spirit? How did the raging sea within him turn to calm waters? For Habakkuk, there was a prayer to pray, a sight to see, and a confession to confess. Let us consider all three.

A Prayer To Pray (3:1-2)

Revival Amid Rebellion

The prayer he prayed is found in the second verse. After telling God he had understood God's promise to discipline Israel with the terrors of a Babylonian invasion and captivity, and that he knew God would eventually judge Babylon, Habakkuk prayed, **"In the midst of years revive it"** (Habakkuk 3:2).

What was Habakkuk asking God to do? What did he want God to revive or renew? Habakkuk was no longer concerned with his own plans but now prayed for God's will to unfold. He wanted God to do a fresh work of chastening and reviving his people. Even though invasion, destruction, and captivity were coming for God's rebellious people, Habakkuk wanted to see revival amid their rebellion. During the **years** of captivity, Habakkuk prayed God would preserve and produce a holy remnant who were all about God and his kingdom.

In a similar way, I believe the chaos and upheaval of our time can be God's instrument to revive his people. We live in a time where God's word and God's church cannot be taken for granted. We must press into both, and the rapidly changing viewpoints of our culture should encourage us to do so. We need the church!

Knowledge Amid Confusion

But Habakkuk also prayed for knowledge to increase during confusing times. He prayed, **"In the midst of the years make it known"** (Habakkuk 3:2). What he wanted here was for God to make believers more knowledgeable about his plans. Many in Israel would stumble at God's plan, just like Habakkuk did, so he wanted God to give them knowledge of his sovereign plans.

In J.K. Rowling's first Harry Potter novel, while Harry is still living with the Dursley family, Mr. Dursley begins seeing strange signs of magic all throughout his day. As a man who hates and disbelieves such things, he is deeply troubled. When he went to sleep that night, he worried Harry's deceased parents were somehow involved, but then comforted himself that he and his wife were safe. Rowling wrote that Mr. Dursley knew that *"it couldn't affect him. How very wrong he was."*[1]

In the same way, how very wrong we are if we think God's discipline could never affect us. It can and often does. And as long as Habakkuk and the people of his day felt they were superior to the Babylonians—and that they could not be affected by God's judgment—they would have a hard time imagining God would discipline them with the Babylonians. So Habakkuk wanted them to have knowledge of their need for God's correction—judgment had to begin at the household of God (1 Peter 4:17).

Mercy Amid Chaos

The last part of Habakkuk's prayer was for God to give them mercy during such chaotic times. He prayed, **"In wrath remember mercy"** (Habakkuk 3:2). The word wrath indicates agitation, excitement, or disturbance. The times they were entering into—invasion, captivity—would be tumultuous. So Habakkuk wanted God to give them his mercy amid all that chaos.

One example of this mercy amid chaos is found in Daniel's three friends. While in Babylon, they were forced to choose between bowing to Nebuchadnezzar's golden statue or burning in a fiery furnace. They told Nebuchadnezzar that they did not know if God would deliver them from the flames or not, but that they did know they could never bow (Daniel 4:17). And when they were thrown into the furnace, God walked with them and indeed preserved their lives. They were given mercy amid chaos.

We, too, can ask God for mercy in tumultuous times. God said, "When you pass through the waters, I will be with you; and through the rivers, they shall not overwhelm you; when you walk through fire you shall not be burned, and the flame shall not consume you" (Isaiah 43:2). Let us pray for that grace to help us endure the times we are in.

Habakkuk prayed his prayer. He wanted God to revive his people during years of chaos, to give them knowledge about his plans for the chaos, and give them mercy to endure the chaos. And we can (and should) ask God for the same.

A Sight To See (3:3-15)

"God came from Teman, and the Holy One from Mount Paran. Selah His splendor covered the heavens, and the earth was full of his praise. His brightness was like the light; rays flashed from his hand; and there he veiled his power. Before him went pestilence, and plague followed at his heels. He stood and measured the earth; he looked and shook the nations; then the eternal mountains were scattered; the everlasting hills sank low. His were the everlasting ways. I saw the tents of Cushan in affliction; the curtains of the land of Midian did tremble. Was your wrath against the rivers, O LORD? Was your anger against the rivers, or your indignation against the sea, when you rode on your horses, on your chariot of salvation? You stripped the sheath from your bow, calling for many arrows. Selah You split the earth with rivers. The mountains saw you and writhed; the raging waters swept on; the deep gave forth its voice; it lifted its hands on high. The sun and moon stood still in their place at the light of your arrows as they sped, at the flash of your glittering spear. You marched through the earth in fury; you threshed the nations in anger. You went out for the salvation of your people, for

the salvation of your anointed. You crushed the head of the house of the wicked, laying him bare from thigh to neck. Selah You pierced with his own arrows the heads of his warriors, who came like a whirlwind to scatter me, rejoicing as if to devour the poor in secret. You trampled the sea with your horses, the surging of mighty waters." (Habakkuk 3:3–15).

The Past

The sight Habakkuk saw is in the bulk of his song (verses 3-15). The bottom line of this part of the song is that Habakkuk had a vision of God, a theophany, a visible manifestation of God's presence. With appropriate veils and imagery, he saw God.

It is a difficult section to interpret with a high level of certainty. One reason for this challenge is that Habakkuk used poetry. Writing with artistic flair, it is sometimes hard to know what events Habakkuk is alluding to with each verse. Is he talking about God's past victory over Egypt? Is he talking about Babylon's future judgment? Or did he have a vision of the ultimate judgment of Babylon in Revelation 17-18?

If this song were a painting, it would not be like da Vinci's Mona Lisa (realism) but more like Van Gogh's Starry Night (impressionism). You know it is a starry night, but its portrayal is quite different than what you see clearly with your eyes in reality. And Habakkuk's prayer does seem to have an impressionistic or kaleidoscoping nature to it—poetic but instructional, clear but transcendent, today but tomorrow, earthly but divine.

It does, however, seem that much of the song is rooted in God's actions in the book of Exodus. In his vision, Habakkuk sees God arriving from **Teman** and **Mount Paran**, a region opposite Babylon, further south than the Dead Sea (3). This was likely a way to stir up memories of God arriving at Mt. Sinai to give Moses (and Israel) the ten commandments and the law (Deuteronomy 33:2).

God's arrival at Sinai was a glorious moment for Israel, filled with lightning, thunder, and the glory of God. As Habakkuk said, **"God's brightness was like the light; rays flashed from his hand; and there he veiled his power"** (4).

Before God came to Mt. Sinai, he had delivered Israel from Egypt with numerous plagues, which is why Habakkuk said that **before him went pestilence** (3:5). And once they wandered in the wilderness for a while, disobedience and sin sometimes released God's direct chastening, which is why Habakkuk said that **plague followed at his heels** (5).

Even the most immovable obstacles were removed at that original Exodus—and their eventual arrival in the Promised Land. As Habakkuk said, God **measured the earth** to give Israel their share and **shook the nations** that got in their way (6). Neighboring tribes and nations—such as **Cushan** and **Midian—trembled** and were **afflicted** (7).

And on the way out of Egypt, God turned the Nile to blood, parted the Red Sea, and held back the River Jordan for his people. But Habakkuk knew that God was not angry with any of those bodies of water. Rhetorically, he asked, **was your wrath against the rivers or the sea, O Lord?** (8). Instead, Habakkuk saw that time of the exodus as a time when God took out his **bow** and **arrows**, causing the earth to **writhe** under the intensity of his work (:9-10). And once they were in the Promised Land, God still induced awe in the way he manipulated nature, causing the **sun and moon to stand still** during the battle of Joshua (11, Joshua 10:12-13).

Remembering all of this about God filled Habakkuk with hope. He is praising God for his past work. He had wondered how God could be so weak as to let the Babylonians be like a fisherman catching fish when he attacked the nations. But with stories from Exodus, Numbers, Deuteronomy, and Joshua in mind, Habakkuk remembered God's strength. God defeated Pharaoh and the nations. He is not weaker than Babylon.

Often, like Habakkuk, we need a fresh vision of God's power. He is not like a kind, old grandfather who is loving yet powerless. Habakkuk sees him here, less like a warm sunset and more like a nuclear shock wave. He sees God as the Sovereign of Sovereigns, the King of Kings.

Is Prologue

God's past work also comforted Habakkuk about his future one. This is where the telescoping nature of his prophecy points forward to God's destruction of Babylon—both the Babylon of his day and the Babylon of our current world system. God's past, in other words, is a mere prologue for what he will do one day.

Our beloved Holdridge family dog is named Max. We found him at the local animal shelter about five years ago. And, though he is a mix, he seems to be mostly Jack Russel Terrier. He has the looks and the feisty trouble-making spirit to prove it.

Recently, I had to take him in because of a little eye condition he could not shake. When his vet came into the room, she was reading his chart while also laughing. When he visits there, it is usually because he endangered himself somehow. He has been there after disturbing a hornet's nest. He has been there after eating a bunch of chocolate. He has been there after eating packs of bubble gum. She was very amused at our little troublemaker.

Well, for Max, the past is prologue. The only way anyone in our house would be surprised the next time he does something naughty is if we forgot his past. But we all fully expect it again because he has done it so many times already.

And—in a much different and holy way—God's past is his prologue. Habakkuk looked back and saw how God judged Egypt and the nations in the Promised Land for their idolatry and evil, so he was comforted that God would do it again. And we can look back, not only at what God did to Egypt, but what God did to Habakkuk's Babylon, and know that God will discipline all nations and drive out all evil one day. His past is his prologue.

God the Rescuer

Habakkuk had clearly fixed his eyes on God with this poem-song of praise. And everything he saw about this Warrior God was that he came to save us. He said, **"You came out for the salvation of your people, for the salvation of your anointed"** (13). That is God's method—he saves us by saving the Anointed One. When Jesus, the ultimate Anointed One, died and was buried and rose again, our victory was secured. Because he rose, we rise!

Habakkuk saw God **crush the head of the house of the wicked, laying him bare from thigh to neck** (13). That is also part of God's method of salvation—he goes after the head. Just as he promised in Genesis, God went after Satan, crushing his head under his feet at the cross (Genesis 3:15).

And Habakkuk saw God **pierce** the enemy **with his own arrows** (14). This is also God's way—he defeats the enemy with their own weapons. We see this in books like Daniel and Esther. Daniel's enemies plotted a way to get him thrown into a lion's den—which he survived. The king was angered by their plot and threw them into the same den—and it did not go as well for them. Esther's enemy was a politician named Haman. He hated all Jewish people because a Jewish man named Mordecai would not bow to him. So he convinced the king to legislate the persecution of Jews on a certain day while constructing gallows to hang Mordecai. Before the day came, however, Queen Esther spoke up. Haman did not know she was a Jew, nor did he know Mordecai was her uncle! The king favored Esther, so he reversed the laws and ordered Haman's death on the very gallows he had built for Mordecai. But we see this most in the cross of Christ—the very instrument the powers of darkness thought would defeat God was used for their own demise!

God is the great rescuer, and it was good for Habakkuk to get his eyes back on God. When he looked at Israel, he was depressed. When he looked at Babylon, he was overwhelmed. But when he looked at God, he was reminded that God has rescued, does rescue, and will rescue.

Martyn Lloyd-Jones pastored in London for many years, including after World War II, when communism was spreading throughout Eastern Europe, and many Christians were deeply concerned. He chose that moment to preach Habakkuk. He said:

> *"It is thoroughly unbiblical and unspiritual to look only at the obviously godless. Christian people and leaders tend to give the impression that there is only one problem—communism. They have fallen into the error into which Habakkuk fell for a while, saying that 'the church isn't perfect, but look at communism; the church isn't all she ought to be, but look at THAT!' They, therefore, see no need for self-humiliation. Many see only one problem, that of the Babylonians—the communists—and so long as they are looking at them, they are not ready to humble themselves."*[2]

Habakkuk had finally humbled himself because he got his eyes back on God. At the beginning of Habakkuk, the prophet reasoned with God in human terms. But now, he is content to let God be God.

***

A Confession To Confess (3:16)

"I hear, and my body trembles; my lips quiver at the sound; rottenness enters into my bones; my legs tremble beneath me. Yet I will quietly wait for the day of trouble to come upon people who invade us." (Habakkuk 3:16).

I Do Not Like It

This leads us, finally, to the confession Habakkuk confessed. In response to his vision of God, he said, **"I hear, and my body trembles; my lips quiver at the sound; rottenness enters into my bones; my legs tremble beneath me. Yet I will quietly wait for the day of trouble to come upon people who invade us"** (16). Augustine once called God the doctor at the core of his being, and here Habakkuk has been shaken to the core of his being by God.

And it appears that Habakkuk has been moved by God but also does not like all that God has said. He is reeling over

God's promise to judge his people and send them into exile in Babylon. The news from God even caused physical sickness and anxiety in God's man.

But I Will Quietly Wait for It

Though he confessed that he was made sick by God's declarations, Habakkuk determined to **wait quietly for the day of trouble to come upon the people who invaded them** (16). He has new resolve as a prophet—he will wait for the day of judgment to come! Though he was pained by the current reality because he had seen God, he was confident in how the story would end.

In 1993, Stephen Spielberg finally won an Oscar for best director. Even though his past movies—*Jaws*, *E.T.*, the *Indiana Jones* trilogy, and even *Hook!*—had massive successes at the box office, his work was not recognized by the Academy. Even *The Color Purple* in 1985 could not get the prized award. But when he released *Schindler's List*, a sober film centered on the Holocaust, the Academy finally thought his work serious enough to receive their praise.

Many attribute his long wait to receive his Oscar to the upbeat nature and happy endings of many of his earlier films. Though the masses loved them, the critics were looking for something real and earthy, something painful and authentic, something free of syrupy sentimentalism.

But could it be that both the popular attraction to a happy ending and the critical desire for a raw story are both right? Could it be that we are meant to both recognize the reality of pain and look forward to the removal of it? Habakkuk entered such a sphere in this prayer. He recognized the pain of today and held fast to the hope of tomorrow. He saw things in the here and now that grieved him, but his vision of God helped him look forward to God's forever kingdom. Habakkuk would even work for life to be better today, all while recognizing it takes God's intervention to solve our deepest ills. He began this book in hopelessness, but he ended it with hopefulness. And he sang this song as a way to renew his hope—writing it down so future generations could use its lyrics to cultivate their own.

Jesus Christ has come with a kingdom. While on earth, Jesus said, "The time is fulfilled, and the kingdom of God is at hand; repent and believe in the gospel" (Mark 1:15). But though his kingdom is here, it is not yet fully here. It is like we are perpetually living life on the Saturday between the cross and the resurrection. The greatness of his work on the cross is available to all right now. But the glory of the final resurrection of his people and the destruction of every rule and authority and power is not yet (1 Corinthians 15:20-25). But, just as surely as the Friday of his cross has come, so will the Sunday of his resurrection when he will "put all his enemies under his feet," including the last enemy, death (1 Corinthians 15:26-27). Though it sometimes feels dark on Saturday, we rejoice that Friday's cross has come, and we trust that Sunday's resurrection will arrive. Sunday is coming.

---

1. Rowling, J. K. 2018. Harry Potter and the Philosopher's Stone. New York, NY: Bloomsbury Children's Books.
2. Lloyd-Jones, Martyn. 1982. From Fear to Faith: Studies in the Book of Habakkuk. Baker Books.

Trust (Habakkuk 3:17-19)

"Though the fig tree should not blossom, nor fruit be on the vines, the produce of the olive fail and the fields yield no food, the flock be cut off from the fold and there be no herd in the stalls, yet I will rejoice in the Lord; I will take joy in the God of my salvation. God, the Lord, is my strength; he makes my feet like the deer's; he makes me tread on my high places. To the choirmaster: with stringed instruments."
(Habakkuk 3:17–19)

We love our transformation stories. Whether a house or a vehicle or a person, we want to be blown away by the finished product. Show us those before and after photos—we are bound to look!

The book of Habakkuk is a song that tells the story of a man who underwent a radical transformation. Here, at the end of his conversation with God, we find a man resolved to trust God no matter what. God had told him that the only way through the years to come was to live by faith (Habakkuk 2:4). This trust in God is still the standard equipment required to navigate our days as well.

Fortunately, Habakkuk pulled out his guitar (**stringed instrument**, 19) and put his story to song, ending with this beautiful bridge. It is meant to stand out because these lyrics demonstrate radical trust in God. Habakkuk has presented the problem (as he sees it) to God, and God has made his promises. Habakkuk has praised God, and now comes the trust. Let us consider the elements of this trust.

Endures Devastation (3:17)

The Fallout of War

First, consider how Habakkuk's trust endured devastation. He said, **"Though the fig tree should not blossom, nor fruit be on the vines, the produce of the olive fail and the fields yield no food, the flock be cut off from the fold and there be no herd in the stalls, yet I will rejoice in the Lord"** (17-18).

These were not hypotheticals in Habakkuk's mind—he believed the ravages of war were coming. With Israel's men engaged in battle, and the families torn asunder by forced relocation, the land would lie barren and the livestock would be untended. It was not a lack of water but rather an abundance of war that would bring them to such conditions. The usual social order that allowed them the time and protections to focus on flocks and crops ended when Nebuchadnezzar began his military campaign against them. The luxury of wine would be one of the first to go, but even Israel's hallmark crops of figs and olives would cease, and the cattle and sheep and goats would no longer produce the meat and dairy to sustain the nation. Israel was told the Promised Land was a land flowing with milk and honey, but the fallout of war would stop the abundant flow of God's good earth.

Acceptance

Habakkuk is unwilling to have his head buried in the sands of oblivion. He is like an accountant, counting every last tragedy to strike the land and considering the far-reaching implications of God's judgment. He has ceased holding out hope for fruit and flocks. Even Habakkuk's basic necessities of life would evaporate—and he knew it.

But Habakkuk is done complaining about it—this is the portion of his song that is resolved and confident in God. He is like Paul the Apostle when he said, *"I count everything as loss because of the surpassing worth of knowing Christ Jesus my Lord. For his sake, I have suffered the loss of all things and count them as rubbish, in order that I may gain Christ"* (Philippians 3:8).

This counting is acceptance. Habakkuk has passed through denial, anger, bargaining, and depression, and now he accepts God's plans of judgment. He is not in denial. He heard the knock of war at the door, and rather than quietly ignore it, he opened the door with a detailed explanation of war's implications.

Picture a child standing at the center of a giant trampoline. Without any momentum, at a total standstill, they cannot get much air. To go high, they first have to go low. Before the trampoline can snap them into the air, they must go low. Before Habakkuk could go up with God, he had to go down into reality.

And Habakkuk certainly did not sound like a victim. As a prophet (and maybe a priest), the indication is that he loved, served, and walked with God. He probably was not guilty of the national crimes God's people had committed, but he was going to go down with them. Yet, even if he had feelings of victimization, he clearly moved past them.

Do not get caught in the cycle of self-pity. We would avoid a lot of our depression, anger, and frustration if we thought about ourselves less. Habakkuk saw the devastation but trusted God would see him through.

The Old Testament record of Job tells of a man who suffered intensely. In a swift moment, he lost everything. His situation was dire enough for his wife to tell him to curse God and die. He refused. He said, *"Should we accept only good from God and not adversity?"* (Job 2:10, HCSB). Job refused the luxury of self-pity, but instead appealed to God's sovereignty. He trusted God.

Esteemed 17th-century pastor Francois Fenelon said there are two kinds of people, "some look at life and complain of what is not there; others look at life and rejoice in what is there." Habakkuk was forced into a situation where he had to respond well to what was not there by rejoicing at who was there—God.

You might be singing Habakkuk's song today. The lyrics are likely a little different—you are not as concerned with figs, olives, cows, or goats, but the tone is the same. *When the addiction is resurfacing...When the marriage is floundering...when the career is flattening...when the church is capitulating...when schools are pronouning...when the teenager is spiraling...when the health is fading...when the inflation is skyrocketing...*

But there is a level of trust in God that can endure every form of devastation. He has been tested through wars and famine, disease and downturn. He is able. He is God. He is good in the midst of all of it.

Finds Joy in God (3:18)

Take Joy

Next, consider how Habakkuk's trust found joy in God. He said, **"I will rejoice in the Lord; I will take joy in the God of my salvation"** (18). His trust in God during devastation was only possible because he found his joy in God. He was not content to only endure the hour of distress—he wanted to pursue God amid all that chaos. **Though** devastation came, **yet** Habakkuk would rejoice in God (17, 18). He was confident that all the hardship could not separate him from his Lord, so he would go **take joy in the God of his salvation** (18).

God had saved them from Egypt and would save them from Babylon, so he called the Lord **"the God of my salvation"** (18). We can say the same of God—he has saved us at the cross and will save us when he returns. He is the God of our salvation, and nothing can separate us from him.

As New Testament believers, we know God this way. After spending the entire book of Romans mining the depths of the gospel, Paul emerged from the mineshaft, took off his headlamp, and proclaimed:

> *"For I am sure that neither death nor life, nor angels nor rulers, nor things present nor things to come, nor powers, nor height nor depth, nor anything else in all creation, will be able to separate us from the love of God in Christ Jesus our Lord."* (Romans 8:38–39)

And because Habakkuk and God were not divided from each other, Habakkuk determined to find his joy in God.

Recently, I was at Asilomar Beach in Pacific Grove, California during sunset, but I was there for something else. Extreme winds created tumultuous but beautiful seas. Watching the waves collide with the rocky shoreline was like watching fireworks explode in the sky. But something else caught my eye. Beyond the rocks was a buoy. Chained to the ocean floor, it was bobbing and reeling like a rodeo star, hanging on for dear life.

For many, the trials and pains of life are like that buoy—just hang on for dear life. The storm has to end sometime, but Habakkuk was not tossed to and fro by the storm at this point. He was transcending the storm, rising above (or beneath) it, going straight to God.

To the Philippians, Paul said, *"Rejoice in the Lord always; again I will say, rejoice"* (Philippians 4:4). Only a believer in Christ could make a statement like that one—no matter what we face, the cross happened. We always have a reason to rejoice in the Lord. In the *"always"* of life, we can rejoice in God.

Rejoice in Him

This level of trust will find its joy in God, as Habakkuk demonstrates, and this generates an inner peace that does not depend on outward prosperity. And this joy is available to anyone because it is based on a person, God himself. Since he always is, and the cross is always true, we can always find our joy in him.

As Augustine prayed: *"This is happy life: to rejoice in your presence, and through you, and because of you. This life is the actual happy life; there is no other kind. Those who think the happy life is different pursue another joy, and not the true one itself."*[1]

In her masterpiece book, *Confronting Christianity*, Rebecca McLaughlin opened with a chapter that asked, "Aren't We Better Off Without Religion?" Many have made this claim. In her response to this charge, she quoted Harvard School of Public Health professor Tyler VanderWeele, who presented "research (that) suggests that those who regularly attend services are more optimistic, have lower rates of depression, are less likely to commit suicide, have a greater purpose in life, are less likely to divorce, and are more self-controlled."[2]

She went on to point out that one of the reasons for this outcome is that believers really can be happy in any circumstance. Like Habakkuk, we can take joy, finding it in God. Some of you—because of atrocities done in the name of religion—might be tempted to say religion is bad for you. But that is like saying drugs are bad for you. Some are, but some are good for you. Some destroy and enslave, but some heal and empower. And for Habakkuk—and many others like him—the knowledge of God has impacted them in positive ways.

For believers, we must fight to believe the right voices, the ones that tell us true satisfaction is found in God. We pray with pastor-author Euguene Peterson:

Deliver me from the liars, God! They smile so sweetly but lie through their teeth. Rescue me from the lies of advertisers who claim to know what I need and what I desire, from the lies of entertainers who promise a cheap way to joy, from the lies of politicians who pretend to instruct me in power and morality, from the lies of psychologists who offer to shape my behavior and my morals so that I will live long, happily and successfully, from the lies of religionists who "heal the wounds of this people lightly," from the lies of moralists who pretend to promote me to the office of captain of my fate, from the lies of pastors who "get rid of God's command so you won't be inconvenienced in following the religious fashions!" (Mk 7:8). Rescue me from the person who tells me of life and omits Christ, who is wise in the ways of the world and ignores the movement of the Spirit.[3]

Gains Strength To Overcome (3:19)

God Is My Strength

Finally, consider how Habakkuk's trust gained him the strength to overcome. He said, **"God, the Lord, is my**

strength; he makes my feet like the deer's; he makes me tread on my high places" (19).

This is the same man who said his legs and whole body trembled, his lips quivered, and rottenness entered his bones (16). He was not strong alone, but after encountering and turning to God, he confessed that God was his strength.

And not only is this strength in contrast to how Habakkuk used to feel, but also to the Babylonian armies. God said, *"Their own might is their god"* (Habakkuk 1:11). For Babylon, their strength was their god. For Habakkuk, God was his strength.

And the strength that God gave Habakkuk remade him into someone able to ascend the heights of victory. Like a mountain deer's muscular frame and sturdy feet, God shaped Habakkuk into a man who could handle the rugged terrain, rise above the chaos, and get to the safety of the **high places** (19).

In the original Matrix movie, Keanu Reeves plays Neo, a messianic figure who will deliver humans from their machine captors. But to enter into the machine's world, he has to be reprogrammed with abilities he would not have previously known. In one scene, he is hooked up to computers that enable him to download (and learn) thousands of fighting styles in only a moment. When he awakes from the download, in surprise, he says the iconic line, "I know Kung Fu."[4]

Habakkuk is saying that he has turned to God, and now he knows Kung Fu. He was not strong, but now he is. God has given him the sturdy feet and a robust cardiovascular system needed to ascend the highest hills. He is weak no more.

Many cyclists and runners use an activity tracking app called Strava. It has all the typical features—pace, distance, elevation, heart rate—but its addictive feature is its "segments," well-traveled stretches of trail or road where so many ride or run that they can provide a leaderboard, even breaking it up by fastest of the day, month, year, or all-time. When I used to do more trail running, I set my sights on Mt. Tallac in Lake Tahoe. Each summer I would peruse those lists to see where I might set my targets. I might not be the fastest up the mountain, but maybe I could beat the other guys my age.

But to get up that mountain, training was required. Over long miles and climbs, my lungs were built up for that annual run-up Mt. Tallac. Without the training, I could never set a decent time.

Here, Habakkuk has been trained by God. The dialogue between man and God, prophet and Lord, hadn't altered God, but it had dramatically changed Habakkuk. Because he brought his problem to God, because God gave him a promise, and because Habakkuk responded in praise, this mountain climbing trust in God was developed. God made him someone and something he was not when the conversation started. He was made fit to go high.

Conclusion

Habakkuk began his book at the lowest of lows. He struggled to understand why God's people were so weak and lawless, as they had clearly rejected God as their King! But then the prophet went even lower when God announced his solution to Israel's spiritual apathy. The Babylonians were coming—a terrible nation would invade a spiritually rebellious one. God would use a violent people to chasten the people he loved. This news sank Habakkuk further into the slough of despond.

But, by the end of the book, Habakkuk is up on the mountain heights. If there is no fruit or flocks, then the prophet will be unmoved because he has God as his joy and strength. God had told him that the only way the righteous can endure such times is by faith, and now Habakkuk is strong in the substance.

As students of his prophecy, we have a decision. Will we walk by sight or by faith? To walk by all we hear or read or witness—by sight—is like trying to walk through quicksand. The more you move, the more entrenched you become. Most of us have had this experience—every day brings a fresh onslaught of news and reports that can draw us deeper down into frustration, anger, or despondency.

But to walk by faith—to trust that God is at work and is enough for us—is like walking on the mountaintops. There, the air is fresh, the water is pure, and the vistas are magnificent.

And we have a choice—quicksand or mountaintops? Sight or faith? People or God? Where will you set your eyes?

When you are open and honest with loved ones, what bubbles forth? Is it fear, anger or depression? Is it a rehashing of the planet's broken people doing broken things? Is it a shocked and befuddled retelling of the old story of the fall and depravity of man?

Or is it faith and hope and joy? Is it a retelling of God's glorious kingdom story, a redeeming God doing redemption things? Is it a calm and soothed retelling of the old story of God's rescue at the cross, filled with confidence that the story is not yet concluded?

Every day, let us join the prophet, departing with him from the quicksand of hopelessness and climbing to the mountains of trust. Christ is there, patiently redeeming and waiting and working, fulfilling the "plan of God for the fullness of time to unite all things in him, things in heaven and things on earth" (Ephesians 2:10). Each day and each moment that the quicksand-ish discouragement seeps in, let us present the problem to God, hear his ultimate promise of redemption, praise him for who he is, and begin to, like Habakkuk, trust again. Because what God announced to this ancient prophet is still true today: *the righteous will live by their faith* (Habakkuk 2:4).

1. Of, Augustine. 2018. Confessions. New York: The Modern Library.
2. McLaughlin, Rebecca. Confronting Christianity. S.I.: Crossway, 2019.
3. Peterson, Eugene H. 1989. Long Obedience in the Same Direction. Glasgow, Scotland: HarperCollins Distribution Services.
4. Wachowski, L., & Wachowski, A. (1999). The Matrix. Warner Bros.

About Nate

Nate Holdridge has served as pastor of Calvary Monterey on California's central coast since 2008. Calvary's vision is to see Jesus Famous. Nate writes and teaches with that aim at nateholdridge.com. He and Christina have been happily married since 2002, and are the proud parents of three incredible daughters.

Books

Podcasts

Jesus Famous Podcast
Through The Bible Series Podcasts
Calvary Monterey Podcast

Bibliography

- Boice, James Montgomery. 2006. *The Minor Prophets: Micah–Malachi*. Ada, OK: Baker Books.

- Bruckner, James. 2010. *Jonah, Nahum, Habakkuk, Zephaniah*. Kentwood, MI: Zondervan.

- Carson, D. A., R. T. France, J. A. Motyer, and G. J. Wenham. 1994. *New Bible Commentary: 21st Century Edition*. Leicester, England; Downers Grove, IL: Inter-Varsity Press.

- Lloyd-Jones, D. M. 2003. *From Fear to Faith: Rejoicing in the Lord in Turbulent Times*. Nottingham, England: Inter-Varsity Press.

- Redmond, Eric, William Curtis, and Ken Fentress. 2016. *Exalting Jesus in Jonah, Micah, Nahum, Habakkuk*. Edited by David Platt, Daniel L. Akin, and Tony Merida. Holman Reference.

- Robertson, O. 1990. *The Books of Nahum, Habakkuk and Zephaniah. The New International Commentary on the Old Testament*. Grand Rapids, MI: Wm. B. Eerdmans Publishing Co.

- Rydelnik, Michael, and Michael Vanlaningham, eds.

2014. *The Moody Bible Commentary*. Chicago, IL: Moody Press.

- Smith, James E. 1994. *The Minor Prophets. Old Testament Survey Series*. Joplin, MO: College Press.

- Smith, Ralph L. 1984. *Word Biblical Commentary. Dallas: Word, Incorporated* 32.

- Tremper, Iii, and David E. Garland. 2008. *The Expositor's Bible Commentary: Daniel–Malachi*. Edited by The Expositor's Bible Commentary 8.

- Walvoord, John F., and Roy B. Zuck. 1985. *Dallas Theological Seminary. The Bible Knowledge Commentary: An Exposition of the Scriptures*. Wheaton, IL: Victor Books.